Best wishes

Dermot-

DERMOT O'BRIEN

Small World

Haiku on The Way

VERITAS

Published 2004 by
Veritas Publications
7/8 Lower Abbey Street
Dublin 1
Email publications@veritas.ie
Website www.veritas.ie

ISBN 1 85390 703 0

10 9 8 7 6 5 4 3 2 1

A catalogue record for this book is available from the British Library.

Designed by Colette Dower
Printed in the Republic of Ireland by Betaprint Ltd, Dublin

*Veritas books are printed on paper made from the wood pulp of managed
forests. For every tree felled, at least one tree is planted, thereby renewing
natural resources.*

AMDA

for

All on The Way

CONTENTS

INTRODUCTION

Many years ago, in search of a form in which to write, I came across the work of Matsuo Basho in an English translation. While reading this I conceived the form in my own mind. Some months later – out of various matters of interest – came the idea of a micro-poetic way towards God.

These taken together offered a programme to be followed. The haiku form in its simplicity and directness and its close association with nature presented a foundation; the direction towards God gave the aspiration. The Zen Buddhist background to the Japanese way was not native to me, although a few years study of it, and an attempt to live it, did yield an enlightenment which I had not experienced before.

However, pursuing the matter, I came to the conclusion that in the Christian tradition there was another opening into the uncreated light of the supernatural, namely, God. And in this, not only nature, but human nature and the Divine were available. In the person of Jesus Christ, the Son of God become man, all three natures were to be found. As the Word of God, Jesus was the origin of creation, nature and human nature, and in himself he is divine.

Furthermore, in a world where much is awry – distorted by the force of evil – here is someone who has within him the power to recover the original innocence of everything. By his life, words, actions, death and resurrection, he demonstrated himself what he described as the Way the Truth and the Life. One of his closest disciples, Saint John, described in his latter years, the vision in which at the end of time all of creation would be restored in Christ.

As part of nature ourselves, and dependant on it, it is a given which we cannot evade. But it is more, because created by God it inevitably reveals something of its maker to us. To those like Saint Francis of Assisi the whole of creation is a revelation of God, something which he set in verse in his 'Canticle of the Sun'. Down through the ages numerous people have been aware, to a greater or lesser degree, of this numinous quality of nature.

The human is conscious of this by virtue of his or her nature, which is at a higher level having been created in the image of God. In his light we see light – the light of the sun, moon and stars and all the other lesser lights we see. And beyond this, by the light of reason, we can see more, and beyond that again we can, by virtue of the light of faith, with the eye of the soul, see even the immaterial – at present very partially, and only by the grace of God, from time to time. Glimpses.

The awareness of reality at whatever level is often momentary. The consciousness that sees clearly comes and goes quickly and it is for the apprehension of such insights, or interpenetrations, that the haiku is an ideal form. Like stepping stones across a stream, they afford a foot-hold in the flux of time. A moment of grace. At least a pointer to ultimate reality; God, our ultimate home.

The Sun in the West

Dead among the leaves
a cock pheasant   its plumage
the grace of Autumn

Traffic taken up
onto another plane   Christ
the goal of it all

The sun in the West
adding a haze to the hills
a way beyond time

Landing in stubble
a flock of starling vanish
briefly to rise again

11

A late afternoon
the quarter moon already showing
the tractors saving beet

In the bare tree-top
the starlings in conference
enjoy the late sun

Like a new laid carpet
the field of wheat already green
below the white house

Gap leading to gap
the fields in November   all
the harvest gathered

The long dead artist
who once flourished in this place
his work now on show

The bramble leaves now
like exotic butterflies
yellow and vermilion

Yawning at the wheel
on the last call of the day
the moon in the sky

The collapsed roof-top
of an abandoned farm-house
cob-webs in the windows

The geese in the yard
suddenly alarmed   somewhere
behind the clutter

Beyond a hedge row
beet tumbling into a truck
ready to move out

A basket of fruit
pumpkins, apples and nuts
placed among straw bales

Of similar hue
the moon and cloud across the sky
towards November's end

The end of the year
a country boy made of straw
proclaims Hallow'een

The rain on the roof
a welcome patter   when all
within weatherproof

For those out of doors
and without a home   a prayer
to God to shield them

Equal before God
every human being   all by
divine grace redeemed

Still to be cycling
when all the world goes by car
resurrects the past

Fast down a steep hill
an old man finds again
the laughter of his youth

Sprinting onto a field
in the best of form   ready
to take on the world

Late in his career
he rises high to catch a ball
and put it over the bar

To see the cup raised
for the fifteenth time   in little
over a century

Those championship days
with all to play for   the county
alive with colour

The balance deciding
over the times of grief   joy
wins out in the end

Gathering the fans
on All-Ireland day   the stations
with train after train

This native county
from hill to horizon   proud
of its representatives

The walk across town
with confidence flying   flags
being waved to and fro

More convivial days
when people stopped on the road
to talk to their friends

Those days when the skill
surpasses historic heights   play
reaches to the heavens

The small county schools
abandoned by the cross-roads
left to fall apart

The long aftermath
in the wake of victory   songs
composed for posterity

From home to a school
of not much greater proportions
the turf on the fire

All through the winter
the days of rain and biting wind
the cup on native ground

The trees of springtime
seen to come into leaf   flowers
in the month of May

Those trees by the road
flowering in May   remembered
the Mother of God

A place to evolve
slowly with the season's   grace
by the way of nature

The year they were built
proudly figured on the wall
slowly begins to fade

Instead of mass-man
with his confrontations   shares
in making bullion

The heart of the world
the heart of Christ   its maker
who made it worthwhile

The nest in a hedge
built last summer   among leaves
that have flown away

The life in all things
at the heart of matter   Christ
who gives them their breath

Ask of the flowers
across a meadow in June
how you came to be

The feeling for life
is the nature of God   love
for the smallest creature

How it lives at all
the insect that alights here
nameless on this page

And if so sparrows
how much more you   who wonder
at the Milky Way

Your heart will tell you
the answer to this   love
that gives joy to life

It's the face of Christ
the complexion of the world
tanned by summer sun

Dressed up for Autumn
a child of straw   makes the case
that all shall be well

An Alpine meadow
in such profusion   the flowers
below the mountain

Above the chimney
a scattering of stars
fires that never fade

The tangle of colour
of petals of all shapes   scents
you never imagined

Between them the word
'peace'   written on a book
the Trinity enthroned

The venue of nature
from sea to mountain   the birds
that bank on the wind

The end of the day
blowing out the candles   the church
locked up for the night

One remains alight
to indicate the presence
of God thro' the night

Dressed for the occasion
a man of straw   in Autumn
surveys the harvest

As if to say look
the dressed up figure of straw
fruit about its feet

Within the context
of everyday life   Christ
makes an appearance

Could you number them
the eyes of children   open
to the world about

Seated at a bar
two friends in conversation
nothing at all withheld

The blind who leave home
to walk to work   trusting
they will find their way

The voice in the cloud
on the summit of the mountain
God to all man-kind

A golden Labrador
walking slowly   accommodates
her sightless master

Changed on the mountain
the appearance of the Lord
Jesus, Son of God

Another nature
in the ascendant   briefly
the Lord transfigured

Evil's frustration
to learn the nature of God
Christ entering hell

A luminous white
never before seen on earth
the colour of His robe

From the unlit grave
to the colour of heaven
those who die in Christ

The last assurance
before the ultimate hour
Christ on Calvary

Four small casseroles
taken from the oven   love
in The Red Café

Contending forces
of good and evil   evil
seaming victorious

Carried down river
the terns on the Slayney   after
the recent drownings

All those long entombed
cut off from the light   awakened
by the voice of Christ

Another river
after time will carry them
with mercy to God

Once there was a king
who understood what it was
to raise all to God

Stark in a bare tree
silhouetted birds   silent
as the sun goes down

Walking the wet street
a disturbed man   conversing
with no-one in sight

After days of rain
the clouds break up   a rainbow
spanning the landscape

The sound of a train
rattling southward thro' the night
the moon slowly rising

Transformed bread and wine
become the body and blood
of Christ its maker

Christ the only King
who lived, died and rose again
serving his people

A motionless mouse
forlorn on the grass   its back
matted by the rain

Farewell those summers
passing in cumulus clouds
stars without hindrance

The cows on the hill
after release from the shed
the milk in the churns

The red and yellows
of the nasturtiums in their bed
lapping a white-washed wall

Embalmed with spices
and enfolded in linen
Christ laid in a tomb

Bread in a griddle
suspended over the fire
rising in silence

The breath of all things
breathed in Christ   living
in the eternal

The jig-saw puzzle
each piece its place   revealing
the finished landscape

Recognised by name
the once despised prostitute
now alive in Christ

The brunt of evil
taken on Calvary   Christ
slowly suffocating

The beauty of those
who believe in Christ   laughter
born of paradise

Appearance on earth
the living and the dead   Christ
is alive for-ever

A water-logged pitch
the end of November   play
postponed indefinitely

Slieve Buí in winter
the sun shafting thro' the clouds
the Wexford landscape

Blessing the houses
the homes of people   everything
within thirty miles

The beauty of Christ
in those He loves   the laughter
born of paradise

The force of the wind
on a Winter's day   the challenge
of God on the heights

Seeing the county
from the summit of Slieve Buí
the sun selected fields

The light within homes
the Light of Christ come to Earth
residence so small

The humblest of hearths
fit enough for Christ   places
where the human survives

Your life on the street
your social life in a lane
seated with some friends

The kindness of Christ
shown to all   manifesting
his presence on Earth

Seated by the door
a traveller shown respect
treated as if Christ

Weather-worn faces
of women not yet old   lives
spent by the road-side

As if waiting for me
long since promised   the Saviour
come down from heaven

Former-generations
evicted from their homes   the road
has become their life

In their hearts alive
the love of Christ   travellers
on their way to God

Your property nil
your insurance non-existent
have-nots of the world

The unnamed magus
who came from the East   delayed
by Christ on the way

The genius of one
who descended to find there
Christ himself disguised

Meeting Him today
at the still centre   the heart
where He waits hidden

The seasons' passing
the years they grow old   in time
till the end arrives

The face of the dawn
in mid-winter   the pink clouds
in the eastern sky

Lazarus by name
who went unnoticed   seated
by the side of God

Somewhere to the East
the blue of the sea   mirrors
the blue of the sky

In providence lived
the life of Christ   opens the hearts
of those who meet Him

As an icon tells
of a divine intuition
God in part present

If all is of God
and God is love ,no wonder
Christ is in all things

The light and darkness
day and night alternating
the sun and the stars

Such shades of colour
blue and green   rose in the East
as the sun rises

The end of the year
a light on in the kitchen
wellingtons at the door

Pink spars in the sky
before sunrise   the school-bus
on a country road

Following the soul
the pianist Alfred Brendel
playing Franz Schubert

When the heart of Christ
finds a home on Earth   someone
is blessing the world

Singing to herself
as she goes about the house
her dream still alive

Coming in Glory
at the end of time   The Lord
Jesus victorious

Temptation still comes
but no longer plausible
the works of Satan

Against the spirit
the waves of illusion contend
fall and die away

The edge of a scythe
tapered like the moon   singing
through the mid-day meadow

A life beyond time
the person you are   spirit
in the eyes of God

This borne flesh and blood
transfigured for eternity
the unique of God

Figures in heaven
recognisable as people
characterised by love

Water from the well
hidden among brambles   haws
the green of summer

Sparks from a grind-stone
the ringing of steel   a song
for the sharpening of blades

The grace of their fall
before the chattering mower
hay swathes in the sun

The banked up river
from the bed of silt   in June
the flowers waist-high

The swathe after swathe
until nothing stands   save the
foxgloves by the ditch

A row of poplars
between meadows by the river
leaves singing in June

One by one the cocks rise
the count of ten, twenty   twenty-five
shaped against the rain

Walking between swathes
laid down in the sun   the stems
of grass and wild flowers

The sound of a train
in late afternoon   its time
to gather in the cows

Milk in a bucket
the cream rising to the top
in the cool of the kitchen

The dew on the fields
of early morning   the tracks
the cows make to the shed

Around the meadow
the horse-drawn wheel-rake sweeps
as if in a dream

Innocence restored
by the grace of God   the fields
as I remember them

The house of the past
still standing in memory   light
pouring through the window

The wounds shall be healed
by the blood of the lamb   grace
the salve from above

The wonder at God
in a miraculous outcome
water become wine

The action of God
creating the Universe
stars in their making

The remotest isle
struck by sunlight   suddenly
become an Eden

The grace from above
the regard of God   changes
all into his peace

A sky in winter
after weeks of rain   revealed
the pink of morning

Hung

with

Raindrops

Knowledge of sources
the one source God   is wisdom
in invisible play

The clear of the blue
before the sun rises   the sky
as on the first day

Before evil was
innocence with God   the sport
of delight in being

The power of God
fashioning beauty   the stars
like scattered diamonds

Born to be playful
all things young   the nature
of God in the world

The dextrous hand
of the love of God   from air
creates a living soul

Ramifications in time
it seems without end   in Christ
leading back to heaven

Play the beginning
of life in a garden   lambs
in the green of Spring

Out of nowhere grace
the overflow of God's love
turns a life around

The homeward journey
of the prodigal child   hurt
at last into sense

Half-way on the road
with nowhere in sight   the halt
to question the heart

Till the shadow fall
and unease creeps in   somewhere
a back turned on God

As a fledgling bird
will cry from the same place
waiting on its mother

Trusting in providence
eternity over time   life
in the care of God

The still point of all
around which everything moves
is the love of God

Name above all names
the Lord of all   the person
of Christ born on earth

Swirling in the light
of a foggy evening   smoke
from an unseen chimney

In his name   our names
becoming divine   adopted
through love of a lamb

The full gift of Christ
a place in heaven   his life
the price that was paid

A night without stars
the country shrouded in fog
lights disembodied

A silent black-bird
silhouetted in a tree
the distant morning star

On a foggy night
the street-lights anchorless
a robin starts to sing

All afternoon long
they rise and fall   the starlings
over the bare fields

The castle-tower
grey in the street-lights
of another world

Announced by angels
and a miraculous star   light
from another world

Gold, frankincense, myrrh
laid on the straw in the cave
where the child is asleep

Beyond human sense
short of the glory of God
the miraculous here

Kings from the Far-East
at the end of their journey
lay aside their crowns

What always has been
the mind of God   breaking in
once more upon man

Another kingdom
beyond the limits of earth
in this child exists

Looking to heaven
the shepherds in the field   lead
the thoughts of all to God

Cypress and olive
growing on the hills   aware
of a light in the dark

Revered once again
the belief in goodness   God
the Son in our midst

Laid down in the straw
the hope of the world   sleeps
like a normal child

Trailing thro' the dark
the lights along the street   lead
towards the tree of life

Never forgotten
the dream of God   in His time
rekindled again

The colour in bulbs
on millions of trees   the world
in festival mode

Old dreams awakened
by the song of angels   choirs
soaring towards the stars

Rejoicing in God
made palpable on Earth   here
take this child to heart

In a troubled world
this shining star   is the hope
of all everywhere

The wide open arms
of an innocent child   touched
the heart of the world

The pride and the joy
of a young woman   Mary
the Mother of God

Away to the North
a mountain-side under snow
promise in the sun

Selected by the sun
that mountain among many
pristine under snow

The work on the hills
in the fertile plain   lessons
that point to heaven

Immersed in water
the Son of God   is with us
here on the planet

Wholly identified
with the lot of mankind   Christ
descended to serve

Leaving Nazareth
the shelter of home   He assumes
his home in Heaven

The Kingdom of God
made present on Earth   in Christ
matter made holy

The familiar paths
become the way to Glory
this world mirrors God

The words from His mouth
raising the dead   Lazarus
after days in the tomb

The earth made ready
to receive the seed   scattered
the largesse of God

Meeting on the road
the ten ostracised lepers
His compassion cures them

Every ear of corn
telling the story of seed
multiplied in the sun

Overlooking the sea
a crowd on a hill   hear Christ
reveal the Kingdom

The dust of the earth
moistened with saliva   cures
a man born blind

The world upside-down
is the way of God's love   poor
to inherit heaven

Hearing in Christ's speech
a voice never before heard
the straight road to God

This promise on Earth
of life eternal   guaranteed
by God in the flesh

A man among tombs
benighted by demons   meets
in Christ a Saviour

A treasure on Earth
the Son of the Eternal
death's end abolished

Humbly beginning
the work of salvation   Christ
on the roads of dust

The endless walking
from village to village   days
in the light of God

The nights under stars
spent in prayer   conversation
with God in heaven

Songs in Paradise
endlessly inventive   sung
to the glory of Christ

The miracles he worked
by the power from on high   Christ
accepted with joy

Gratitude his song
as all was being accomplished
even death on the cross

The ultimate task
accepted with confidence
He gave his life away

The names being called
like peals of joy   until all
have made their way home

Three days of darkness
then the glory of heaven
time become forever

The billion loose ends
all drawn together   God
reveals His glory

Each in the other
the Three Divine Persons   shine
with the bliss of God

The victory of God
love itself   the Trinity
who embraces the world

A light so radiant
it encompasses all   God
in the midst of creation

A house abandoned
crumbling by the road-side   gone
the once inhabitants

Music and dancing
sport and creation   celebrate
the mastery of God

Bleating in the fields
as if always there   the first
lambs of the new year

Sheltered by evergreens
the new thatch on a farm-house
fresh after winter rains

Stooped in his garden
an old man no longer hears
the passing traffic

The pearl of great price
at last made perfect   contains
the sum total of God

Facing south-westwards
the rooks in the tree-top   sense
the coming of spring

The broken arches
where once the aisles   surrounded
the ancient abbey

Standing by the tree
the ruined tower of the abbey
equal in winter

Five lancet windows
all that remains standing now
of the antique church

Gathered together
a few of Christ's disciples
share a late supper

Pencil slim windows
of the restored cathedral
catch the rising sun

Hung with rain-drops
the willow now   prepares
for another spring

There on the summit
of Mt Tabor   Christ, Moses
and the prophet Elijah

Summoning to mind
the figure of Christ   seated
in the shade of a tree

A solitary plane
across a field of stars   the sound
it leaves in its wake

The nights in the hills
alone in prayer with God   the stars
the floor of heaven

In wind-driven rain
Christ on the hill of Calvary
the desolation

The coming of dawn
the chorus of birds   begins
his day of blessing

Confidence of faith
on a raw day in winter
summer will return

The connection made
between heaven and Earth   Christ
the goodness of God

The calm that He brought
to all whom He met   fearless
the Son of Heaven

Along the road-way
the blind as He passed cried out
Lord that we may see

See you in the flesh
that we may see into you
you who come from God

Whatever the disease
that troubled the afflicted
you could take away

All who came in faith
He received with compassion
his touch healed them all

Children you favoured
for their innocence   their trust
their straight-forward love

Being in their presence
was like being at home   truth
in all of their eyes

The steps by a well
a place you could sit   aware
of the water of life

What seemed like random
the encounters you had   were
planned before time began

Already on Earth
the knowledge of God   the keys
to The Kingdom granted

A short conversation
with an ostracised woman
brought her home to God

That she could be loved
by the love of God the Father
utterly and forever

The stigma of blame
of ill repute   in a trice
totally removed

Born to know The Lord
at three she thought of heaven
sitting by a stream

Meeting in The Lord
the Son of God   the transport
to the land of joy

Growing rapidly
she soon encountered the fact
of death here on Earth

A meeting in truth
without pretence   without lies
wholeness recovered

The wisdom of God
given her early   she knew
the value of suffering

As a child of eight
the forthrightness of her look
Thérèse of Lisieux

To set others free
to find their destiny   in God
for whom they were born

Her name in the stars
she found in childhood   the road
her short life would take

Enduring the pain
physical and spiritual
the road to Calvary

Her love in response
to the love of Christ   her gift
to the rest of the world

Her desire in love
to reach the whole world   given
long after her death

The suffering of Christ
she interpreted correctly
all borne for others

Travelling the world
her mortal remains   brought forth
the mercy of God

The silence of death
become eternal eloquence
doctor of the church

Her genius to know
God as a loving father
she went to like light

The light of a child's love
direct as an arrow   launched
from a guileless heart

For across the plain
the town of Ferns   the ruins
among new houses

Among the great saints
those who loved much   St Thérèse
has taken her place

Someone to call on
in time of need   she answers
with the grace of God

Fields without cattle
without sheep   only the wind
racing through the grass

Seen from a window
small birds in the garden   sweep
by on outstretched wings

Sheltered in a barn
the cattle   out of the wind
graze on ample hay

The drama of God
the sunlight in the tall trees'
silent radiance

Out of the Bible
the infant Jesus   appears
to St Anthony

An

Ember of

Truth

White pink and orange
the streetlights after midnight
traffic far away

To the pure of heart
all things are pure   Creation
is the work of God

The years that have flown
since Patrick was a shepherd
the moon over Saul

A winter landscape
all the ploughed fields and bare trees
the water-logged gaps

The moon over Saul
on a clear night   St Patrick
at home in heaven

Beneath the bright stars
a boy on a hill   sensing
the nearness of God

Growing so quickly
on a foreign hill   Patrick
in the love of God

Above the street-lights
of a small town   the stars
shining in silence

The pearl among stars
his new found knowledge of God
on a cold hill-top

The prayer he had learnt
as a child at home   exiled
now brings him to God

Rescued from the mud
to be placed high on a wall
he sees the whole world

After his escape
grown to maturity   he hears
the call to return

The order of God
one and three-fold   eternal
above mortality

Inspired to leave all
his home in Wales   his people
in response to God

The years of study
in the south of France   over
he sails for Ireland

Knowing the landscape
he went to Tara   lighting
the fire of intent

Something enkindled
so long lying dormant   fire
of the original God

Amazing the King
by defying protocol   blazing
the fire of a new order

The Son of The Lord
come down from heaven   born
a child in Bethlehem

Certain in his faith
he persuaded so many
to receive the grace of God

The Good News travelled
moving Westwards in the heart
of a man redeemed

A promise so great
it lifted his bearers   high
among the angels

The hills of Ireland
his given command   with love
he worked for The Lord

God as a father
someone who could be met with
through the grace of Christ

Profound in his faith
his knowledge of God   Patrick
brought here to Ireland

The greatest of gifts
the gift of heaven   he gave
to all who would hear

The Spirit inspired
the words that he spoke   water
pouring upon heads

His courage immense
his faith unshakeable   Patrick
spent himself for God

Beyond all measure
this grace of God   transmitted
by a simple man

In his own words unschooled
he feared the learned   yet in him
was the power of God

For centuries now
his legacy has lasted
a plant still alive

At the hour of death
a gateway to Paradise
St Patrick opens

The truth about God
among myriad angels
the song of heaven

A light for today
it still flares the providence
only God can grant

Parades and marches
around the world   St Patrick
honour with gladness

A glowing ember
all that remains of a faith
begun long ago

The conductor God
of supreme intelligence   grace
His measureless love

An ember of truth
about to be rekindled
a flame once again

Culminating time
all things recapitulated
find themselves in God

The wonder of grace
in the end made manifest
rainbows round the world

Against a Blue Sky

Asleep on a bus
people from the morning ferry
travelling on to Dublin

Cosmos in motion
to the eternal music
in heaven composed

Spring along the hills
the rising sun now catches
the evergreen pines

Radiance everywhere
the expression of joy   God
in all his creatures

Swaying in the breeze
of early March   the cherry-tree
beginning to flower

The one-time artist
become a saint   thro' visions
of another world

About to open
the leaves on the willow-tree
the stars far away

The band-stand at dawn
only a nearby fountain
is still pumping life

All gone   so many
those who once sang on earth
sing beyond the stars

Whatever their themes
their cast of mind   a new world
has opened for them

The glory of God
manifest on a mountain   Christ
on earth as in heaven

A great hope realised
the smile of someone dying
into eternal life

A foretaste of spring
a butterfly wanders alone
over a ploughed field

Directly overhead
'The Plough' moved into position
the sound of traffic

A blue sky at dawn
the leaves about to open
on a chestnut tree

The white bandaged head
of a child in hospital
the fear in her eye

Beyond the castle
the far-off Black Stairs Mountains
seen thro' a spring haze

Out of a corner
a pheasant caught by surprise
suddenly in flight

Leaving the main road
the endless din of traffic
the by-roads in spring

Slowly dissolving
the trail of a jet gone by
in the sun of spring

A corner of a field
churned up in winter   stagnant
with oily water

Waiting in a field
a harrow among the drills
dried by the spring sun

Ready to depart
the jeep and trailer in a yard
for a distant market

A head-land in spring
dry after the winter rains
the grass again grows

Crackling underfoot
the beach-mast on the dry ground
after a rain-free March

Leaning across the road
away form the prevailing wind
the beech-trees in Spring

Among the yellow
primroses by the road-side
almost unseen purple

Along the road-side
primroses almost covered
by the growing grass

Across a vast field
a tractor with fertiliser
all day back and forth

The hedge-rows yellow
with furze along the hill-sides
Wexford in springtime

All winter harshness
disappeared without trace   spring
only in evidence

The sore battered heart
begins to revive   along
with the song of spring

An invisible bee
somewhere on a deserted road
primroses in spring

Against a blue sky
the yellow of gorse in flower
the cool breeze of spring

Even miles away
you see the colour of gorse
the last day in March

Along the road-way
the well-kept cottages   now
bright with daffodils

In Clologue grave-yard
the life-sized figure of Christ
crucified in spring

Beyond all this blue
this passing spring   the Kingdom
that never changes

The door left open
a country school-house in spring
the children gone home

Shining in the sun
the grass in an upland field
the song of finches

Ample places yet
for those still to die   the peace
of this resting place

Landing in the grounds
of a well-kept country church
a solitary pigeon

Beginning to show
the wheat in a hill-side field
the heat of the sun

Above the heather
the raised figure of Christ
the peace of the dead

Flashing in the sun
a plane above Carrigroe
heading away westwards

The last day of March
the dead in the grave-yard lie
mindful of eternity

The colour of flame
a fire in the corner of the field
the last day of March

Completely overgrown
a ruined cottage by the road
the front door missing

Turning steadily
a wind-mill on the hill-side
the prevailing wind

Across a green field
a drop into a valley
the distant mountains

A grass covered hill
rising into a blue sky
nothing else in view

Protecting his face
a farmer burns old rubbish
at the end of March

In a country church
the stillness of a spring day
the Divine presence

The clear ringing song
of birds outside in the grounds
audible in a church

A sole worshipper
in the silence of a church
sits quietly for hours

'Welcome to Ballycanew'
on the road into the town
neatly carved in stone

The bewildered look
of a child injured in war
who could make sense of

A continent away
from the peace of this small church
a day and night war

An affront to God
the wars men wage in His name
children blown to bits

The deepest of red
the gas-fires on either wall
of the church in spring

Beyond all malice
the belligerence of men   God
in heaven's patience

The justice of God
forever in heaven   the grace
of infinite mercy

One by one all come
before the judgement of God
good or ill to tell

Carried to a grave
a four-year-old child   men
proclaim this is war

Someone made ready
this place of worship   prayer
in the presence of God

Down the centuries
the same song of birds in spring
the church doors open

Along the by-roads
the mossy banks   primroses
and other small flowers

Spring seems eternal
when wheat again surfaces
green above the clay

All the way down-hill
the daffodils by the drive
to the farm below

Horses in a field
with mountains in the distance
an air of far away

Those who do not hear
but without God live their lives
live in ignorance

Leaving its four trails
a jet in the clear blue sky
can it sense this spring

The pattern of fields
stretching to the far mountains
all the work of spring

Tossing in the wind
a few garden daffodils
facing towards the sea

Stopped at the head-land
the plough raised up in sunlight
a brief flash of steel

As if neatly combed
the wheat-field about to sprout
will in summer sway

Turning at the head-land
the raised double plough share
before it sinks in earth

Only the roof-tops
visible from the road   a farm
down in the valley

Cutting into the ground
the lowered coulter   a plough
turns the earth over

By late afternoon
the field that was earlier stubble
almost wholly ploughed

Gathering momentum
on the remaining head-land
the sun dropping low

The high powered tractor
drawing up to a head-land
slowly decelerates

About a gateway
the primroses at random
bring the grace of spring

Suddenly piping
a pheasant in the near wood
then silence once more

Along the road-side
trickling uninterruptedly
the water of spring

Below the surface
the long green river-weed
wavers overjoyed

The pain of being used
locked in a loveless marriage
the frenzy to escape

Overnight in spring
the river become transparent
the washed sand below

Hidden in a hedge
the broom until it flowers
yellow in late March

The flood water gone
nothing of that brown torrent
but the dishevelled banks

Only inches deep
the river under the bridge
the play of sunlight

With what grace it sways
the willow tree sprouting leaves
in an evening breeze

In folds to the woods
the fields ascending light-green
already in March

Surprised by a starling
alone on a telegraph wire
its few notes of song

Mothers with children
on the road homewards from school
the lengthening days

End of a spring day
the clouds quickly gathering
a change in the weather

The distant mountains
the limit of a heat haze
beyond which unknown

Making the acquaintance
of a puppy on the road
such great excitement

A stairs to a loft
in the light of spring   gleaming
with a new future

The clocks gone forward
to make the days longer still
warmer weather here

The back of the house
a wall with a climbing rose
that never failed to flower

Around the houses
daffodils everywhere   wild
in their variety

A much used cloth-cap
ever on a farmer's head
the years have turned grey

Across the county
old houses being restored
wooden floors and stairs

With less urgency now
after all the years of sowing
the tractor moves along

The season's passing
and the years with them   others
younger came along

The brand-new tractors
with more powerful engines
young men at the wheel

Fast along the road
the power-tractors in April
work still to be done

How they sweep along
never noticing the flowers
the road-side in spring

The heather in flower
beneath a life-sized crucifix
homage paid to God

The same expression
year after year   of the cross
in a small grave-yard

A flickering light
passed thro' a stained-glass window
the colours of God

Across the garden
in two seconds   a bumble-bee
in the cool of April

From what depths of earth
this igneous stone has come
gleaming with mica

Beneath the rook's nest
droppings spattered on the road
the sunlight of spring

Risen from a head-land
a hen pheasant flies and glides
the length of a field

The hills over hills
and then the distant mountains
vague in a spring haze

The undisturbed bank
of a country by-road   bright
with yellow primroses

An abandoned house
the strawberry shrubs in April
continue to flower

Lying on its side
a pony in a spring field
enjoys the sun's warmth

The trickle of streams
in the dips among the hills
all without a name

The flick of a tail
otherwise motionless horses
in a sun-lit field

Cut from the bank-side
the furze bushes in the stream
beginning to fade

The breeze in its mane
a pony lying on the grass
unwilling to stir

Somewhere to the East
the spring-sea rises and falls
on deserted strands

Half in the sun-light
and half in shadow   primroses
under a hazel-tree

Rolling in the lime
a mare covers herself with dust
them abruptly stands

The old stone bridges
over so many rivers
greet another spring

On a shaded bank
the small white fritillaries
modest in their show

Down in a hollow
the clatter of machinery
carried on the wind

The larch in a wood
already turned a light green
the growth of April

Coming to a halt
a coach at a lay-by
the spring dust rises

The shadow of a gate
slowly moving with the sun
the cool of April

The vale of Carnew
between Wicklow and Wexford
all the fields of spring

Red, yellow and green
the combines in the distance
a festival field

At first it seemed odd
swathes of plastic in a field
the frosts of April

Early day in spring
the harvesters standing still
the months to Autumn

Houses and villages
scattered across the hill-side
in April sun-light

The colours to come
in the lately harrowed fields
green to sun-lit gold

A distant village
the steeple of an old church
the greyness of stone

Overhanging a stream
the primroses in profusion
yellow in April

A regular boom
softened by distance   alarms
the marauding crows

The bleating of lambs
only days old on the hills
travels on the breeze

Poignant the houses
on the distant hill-side   apart
in the same spring sun

In a state of war
the endless lies   propaganda
from both aggressors

The newly built house
in the sun of its first spring
all the years to come

Only the uppermost
branches of a willow   move
in the evening breeze

Out of alignment
the lust for power   without God
it brings corruption

Since all before God
are human beings   no warfare
can be justified

Suddenly disturbed
a cock and a hen pheasant
run into the woods

A gold-crested wren
at the foot of a tree   busy
feeding on insects

The general says
we are making history
corpses everywhere

To keep up with spring
a book of illustrated flowers
tulips now in bloom

The Prime Minister talks
at home with the people   lies
they read in his eyes

Rangeing a hill-side
the sheep with lambs in April
the distance between them

Randomly in ivy
the five petaled mauve flowers
open in April

Observed from the road
the quizzical look of a lamb
a kind of blessing

Such the lamb of God
except Christ knew He would die
to heal the great wound

The power of a bull
grazing peacefully in a field
the new grass of spring

Scrambling playfully
four or five lambs on a bank
a coney near by

To the Graveyard

An orange-tipped white
floating by on the sunlight
and then back once more

Perhaps a mystic
the homeless man who just smiled
watching the clock move

Entering harbour
the great ship reverses engines
coming to itself

Birds in the evening
singing now and then   won't they
be singing in eternity

How high in the wind
can a kite fly   before time
calls in from the dusk

All things loved in time
will be raised hereafter   God
will see to their bliss

Time and eternity
together in the present   now
is the hour of God

A kite on a string
your soul tethered to the Earth
the wind seeks to lift

The presence of God
is always present   seasons
but the coats he wears

Wherever they fly
the kites on a strand   someone
must help them to rise

A vision of the world
shot through with grace   radiance
in the joy of God

A kite among stars
was ever such seen   to dim
the light of heaven

The night time has passed
with its promise of the stars
day becomes forever

The child of wisdom
at the making of the world
knew how all things worked

The figure of Christ
on Tabor once   now always
the heart of the world

Then the singing comes
that was always there   gathered
to the glory of God

Recognition of God
in the faces of all   summoned
to eternal joy

Christ the vanquisher
from the throes of hell   rises
to the peaks of heaven

Stretching out his wings
the Holy Spirit   embraces
all matter with love

Glancing off hill-tops
the sun strikes into the blue
one eternal day

These humble temples
the bodies where He dwelt   shine
with the Glory of God

Radiance in all
in the life always promised
Hosanna in excelsis

Father in heaven
we come to recognise you
the provenance of love

The evening star
between two trees   not yet
come into leaf

For someone this day
will be a defining one
the day death will come

The constellations
from a small town in Ireland
the beginning of spring

A light in the lane
immediately overhead   the moon
near and far away

The sound of a bell
a coffin going from the church
slowly towards the graveyard

The prayers at the end
that seemed to no avail   now
the soul's guidance home

An ordinary day
a resident of the town
carried to the grave

Fingers on a keyboard
with the urgency of a life
a wave's run to shore

The space between lives
those just come and those leaving
all call it heaven

For all that its worth
a thrush sings from a tree-top
the sun going down

Walk of communion
the distance to the grave-yard
a waiting fresh grave

The mercy of God
in a merciless death   Christ
hanging on a cross

The cushion of faith
that enables a cortege
to walk towards a grave

The new creation
on the hill of Calvary
the place of resurrection

Lazarus in the tomb
already decomposing   Christ
summons back to life

The ultimate stop
when Christ died on Calvary
turned into The Way

The recall once more
of the reach of Christ   his death
that won life for all

The threshold of God
in Christ on earth   leads into
the home of the blessed

His head to one side
Christ on the cross   in the end
forgave his enemies

Although crucified
evil could not penetrate
Christ in His father

Before you were born
your identity in God
makes you who you are

Beyond

All

Measure

Haphazardly crossing
a rain-wet lane   the shadows
of rooks from above

Shown to have blossomed
the cross on which Jesus died
the empathy of nature

Barely visible
two lambs beside their mother
in the long-grass

Daisies and campion
primroses and blue-bells
the colours of spring

The wind in a beech
lately unfurled   the lonely
sound of far off springs

Seen at close quarters
the faces of violets   fresh
after a spring shower

The overnight rain
lodged in a gateway wheel-rut
far from a farmhouse

The lane to the woods
still wet from over-night rain
all the small wild flowers

Merging with the clouds
Mt Leinster in the distance
a rainy day in spring

Under a broken sky
the countryside to the horizon
the green of new leaves

Exposed on a bank
the roots of an old oak tree
endless wind and rain

Almost unnoticed
a bank-full of primroses
on a country lane

Looking up the track
beneath the lightly leaved beeches
the array of bluebells

Wherever you look
across the floor of the wood
bluebells in late spring

A welcome in spring
the beechwood with its lower branches
light green leaves unfurled

Overgrown with ivy
a tree no longer recognisable
collapsed into a ditch

Ringing with birdsong
the beechwood in April
the bluebells silent

Swaying against the sky
the tall slender larch trees
in a gentle breeze

As the sun comes out
a small white butterfly appears
wandering through the wood

Such a wood as this
an ideal place to rendezvous
with the risen Christ

The sleeves of yellow
the gorse among the saplings
of evergreen firs

The moss on a log
still damp after recent rain
sun and wind will dry

A mass on a rock
the mountains all around
the clouds overhead

The narrowing track
leading out of the wood-land
grass along its centre

The tips of fir-trees
aspiring to the heights   lonely
under the passing clouds

Gorse between the fields
on the uplands of Slieve Buí
rain clouds passing by

A small meadow-brown
its wings outstretched on a leaf
painted cream markings

As yellow as gorse
the empty fertilizer bags
left in a wheat-field

Among the normal
beech saplings in green   one
in copper unfolds

The dust covered leaves
under the recent rainwater
a long drought ended

Through the beechwood green
a steep bank covered in gorse
flaming bright yellow

The brightest of sprays
the lately unfurled beach-leaves
translucent in the sun

Dappled with sunlight
the floor of a native beechwood
bluebells in profusion

Alone in a haggard
an apple tree in blossom
swallows sweeping by

The remains of a tower
all that stands of an old abbey
across the spring fields

As if slowly sighing
a single broom in the breeze
displays its blossom

The old sexton's house
renovated to become
a meeting place for all

Quaint by the road-side
the old thatched-house restored
young trees in the grounds

Returned to their birth-place
the swallows round the old mill
cut through the spring rain

The end of the month
at last the April showers have come
pattering on the rooftops

Amid the foliage
of the lilac in blossom
a resting blackbird

Across the country
April showers passing onwards
grey in the distance

The sound of hammering
inside a new extension
someone hard at work

A stretch of old road
the grass and various flowers
encroach on the tar

Returned with a spear
Christ having died on the cross
the hatred of men

A pair of gold-finch
preen themselves on a tree-stump
between the April showers

The blood on the cross
the very heart of Christ   becomes
the life of the world

The crow of a cock
on the first morning of May
all the years gone by

Into the body
of the material world   His blood
trickles redemption

Underneath the stars
all the birds have gone silent
the hedge in darkness

Forever victorious
the Son of Man   in heaven
welcomes his friends home

Ultimate malice
directed against Jesus
dead upon a cross

A love so immense
in such humble guise   a friend
is all that he says

Courtesy untold
in the court of heaven   Christ
welcoming His friends

Elevation there
you barely notice   such love
as Christ embodies

Come down from heaven
the Word of God   become man
destroys the work of Satan

Beyond all measure
the love of God   welcoming
his creatures to Paradise

As when from the skies
a jet lands   people applaud
the skill of a pilot

The salve of his grace
absolving all hardship   woe
transformed into joy

The miracle wrought
of all turned around   each one
in the smile of God

I am who I am
in the image of God   as you
are and everyone else

Taken from a hedge
a branch of gorse   lovingly
placed before the Host

Human to divine
the journey of the heart   slowly
returned to its maker

In the end a fount
of pure water   ascending
in the light of spring

The gift of Himself
one hand on his heart   Jesus
holds up the Eucharist

Its nature established
in the joy of its maker
love soars unhindered

On a breath of wind
a bumble-bee crosses the stream
and is gone from sight

Scattered everywhere
the petals from the cherry trees
after a stormy night

After the spring rain
the river in full spate   sings
on its way to the sea

Coiled like seahorses
the bracken along the roadside
about to straighten out

Close to the old bridge
a yellow wagtail perches
on a stone above water

Low over the Bann
the blue-bolt of a kingfisher
quickly lost to sight

Dancing above the stream
the yellow wagtail snatches
flies blown on the wind

Its favourite perch
the wagtail below the bridge
where its nest is hidden

Again and again
it resumes its landing stone
a wagtail in May

Under the stone bridge
a swallow in flight   briefly
the cool of the shade

Its non-stop gurgling
the river over a stoney bed
after the spring rain

In time with the times
the river on its way to the sea
carries all away

There is an ocean
stretching over the horizon
small beneath the sky

To the maker of all
the colour of nature   God
the salute of May

Archetypal white
far across a field   a swan
where the river flows

The palest of mauves
a wild flower in a green field
trembles on the breeze

Silent where its deep
the river flows   past the trees
in the green of spring

Away to the south
the railway runs   between banks
yellow now with gorse

Like apple blossom
the tulip by the doorway
receives the spring rain

The eagles by the door
static in stone   look balefully
on a small garden

Lettered in gold paint
'I am with you', forever
since it comes from God

Communion with God
sitting in a silent chapel
the Eucharist exposed